WHAT IS THE BOOK OF 2 SAMUEL?

Kids' Guides to God's Word Series

What Is the Book of Genesis?
What Is the Book of Exodus?
What Is the Book of Leviticus?
What Is the Book of Numbers?
What Is the Book of Deuteronomy?
What Is the Book of Joshua?
What Is the Book of Judges?
What Is the Book of Ruth?
What Is the Book of 1 Samuel?
What Is the Book of 2 Samuel?
What Is the Book of 1 Kings?
What Is the Book of 2 Kings?
What Are the Books of 1–2 Chronicles?
What Are the Books of Ezra & Nehemiah?
What Is the Book of Esther?
What Is the Book of Job?
What Is the Book of Psalms?
What Is the Book of Proverbs?
What Is the Book of Ecclesiastes?
What Are the Books of Song of Songs & Lamentations?
What Is the Book of Isaiah?
What Is the Book of Jeremiah?
What Is the Book of Ezekiel?
What Is the Book of Daniel?
What Are the Books of Hosea–Micah?
What Are the Books of Nahum–Malachi?
What Is the Gospel of Matthew?
What Is the Gospel of Mark?
What Is the Gospel of Luke?
What Is the Gospel of John?
What Is the Book of Acts?
What Is the Book of Romans?
What Is the Book of 1 Corinthians?
What Is the Book of 2 Corinthians?
What Is the Book of Galatians?
What Is the Book of Ephesians?
What Is the Book of Philippians?
What Are the Books of Colossians & Philemon?
What Are the Books of 1–2 Thessalonians?
What Are the Books of 1–2 Timothy & Titus?
What Is the Book of Hebrews?
What Is the Book of James?
What Are the Books of 1–2 Peter & Jude?
What Are the Books of 1-3 John?
What Is the Book of Revelation?

What Is the Book of

2 SAMUEL?

Michael Whitworth

© 2026 by Michael Whitworth

All rights reserved. No part of this publication may be reproduced, stored in a retrieval system, or transmitted in any form or by any means without the prior written permission of the author. The only exception is brief quotations in printed reviews.

ISBN 978-1-971767-14-7

Published by Start2Finish
Bend, Oregon 97702
start2finish.org

Printed in the United States of America

30 29 28 27 26 1 2 3 4 5

For my cousin Eddy—

Heroes rise and fall.
Jesus Christ is the same yesterday, today, and forever.

CONTENTS

Introduction 9

1. When Your Enemy Falls 15
2. A Seat at the Table 27
3. When the Hero Falls 39
4. The Fire Inside the House 51
5. The King Who Ran 61
6. Still Standing 73
7. The Last Word 83

INTRODUCTION

Have you ever admired someone so much that finding out they failed felt like the ground shifted under your feet?

Maybe it was a coach you looked up to who turned out to be dishonest. Maybe it was an older kid you respected who made a terrible choice. Maybe it was someone in your own family, someone you thought had everything together, and then one day you found out they didn't. That moment when the person you believed in turns out to be deeply, painfully human.

Now hold that feeling and multiply it by an entire nation. That's 2 Samuel.

This book gives us the greatest king Israel ever had at the peak of his power, ruling a united nation, receiving an astonishing promise from God, writing songs of worship that people still sing three thousand years later. And then this same book shows us that king committing adultery, arranging a murder, watching his family disintegrate, fleeing his own capital while his son steals his throne, and burying children who died because of choices he made.

Second Samuel is the story of David. All of David. The best of him and the worst of him, and the God who refused to let go of him through either one.

WHERE WE'VE BEEN

If you've read 1 Samuel, you know the backstory. Israel demanded a king "like all the other nations," and God gave them Saul, a man who looked the part but whose heart was never anchored to God. When Saul's disobedience cost him the throne, God sent Samuel to Bethlehem to anoint a replacement: David, the youngest son of Jesse, a shepherd boy nobody thought to invite inside when the prophet came calling.

What followed was one of the most dramatic stretches in the entire Bible. David killed Goliath. He became a national hero. He married Saul's daughter and became best friends with Saul's son. And then Saul tried to kill him. For years David ran, hiding in caves and deserts, gathering a ragtag band of followers, twice sparing Saul's life when he could have taken it. He waited for God's timing when seizing the throne would have been so much easier.

First Samuel ended in darkness. Saul and Jonathan were dead on Mount Gilboa. The Philistines had won. The nation was shattered. David was still an outlaw, camped in enemy territory, waiting for a kingdom that seemed further away than ever.

Second Samuel picks up right there, and it answers the question 1 Samuel spent thirty-one chapters asking: What happens when God's chosen king finally gets the throne?

The answer is more complicated, more beautiful, and more heartbreaking than anyone expected.

WHAT YOU'RE ABOUT TO READ

Second Samuel covers roughly forty years of David's reign, and the story breaks into two very different halves.

The first half (chapters 1–10) is David at his finest. He mourns Saul and Jonathan with one of the most beautiful poems in the Bible. He becomes king of Judah, then king of all Israel. He conquers Jerusalem and makes it his capital. He brings the ark of the covenant to the city and dances before the Lord with everything he has. God makes an astounding promise: David's throne will last forever, and through his family line, God will bless the world. David defeats every enemy around him and shows stunning kindness to a crippled grandson of Saul, inviting him to eat at the king's table for the rest of his life.

If the book stopped there, it would be an incredible story of faith rewarded.

It doesn't stop there.

The second half (chapters 11–24) begins with one sentence that changes everything: "But David remained at Jerusalem." While his army was at war, David stayed home, and in that idle moment he made the worst decision of his life. He took another man's wife. He tried to cover it up. When the cover-up failed, he arranged the man's murder. And though God forgave David when he confessed, the consequences never stopped coming.

From that point forward, the book becomes a story of fallout. David's son Amnon attacks his half-sister Tamar. David does nothing. Absalom murders Amnon and eventually leads a full-scale rebellion that drives David out of Jerusalem. Civil war erupts. Absalom is killed, and David's grief nearly destroys him. Even after David returns to the throne, the nation is fractured, and more revolts follow.

The book ends not with a triumphant finale but with David on his knees at a threshing floor, offering a sacrifice to stop a plague his own foolishness caused, at the very spot where Solomon will one day build the temple.

WHY THIS BOOK MATTERS

You might be thinking, "This sounds depressing. Why should I read a book about a hero who fails?"

Because the Bible isn't interested in giving you heroes who never fail. It's interested in showing you what God does with people who do.

Second Samuel matters because it's honest. It doesn't airbrush David. It shows you a man who wrote Psalm 23 and also wrote a letter ordering an innocent man's death. It shows you that spiritual greatness and moral failure can live in the same person. And it refuses to let you be comfortable with either one. You can't read 2 Samuel and walk away thinking sin doesn't matter, because the consequences are devastating. But you also can't walk away thinking failure is the end of the story, because God's grace is relentless.

Second Samuel also matters because at its center stands one of the most important promises in the entire Bible. In chapter 7, God tells David that his dynasty will last forever. That promise echoes through every prophet, every psalm, every genealogy in Scripture. It's the reason the angel told Mary her son would sit on "the throne of his father David." It's the reason Matthew opens his Gospel by calling Jesus "the son of

David." The promise God made in 2 Samuel 7 is the thread that connects the Old Testament to the New, and it leads straight to the manger, the cross, and the empty tomb.

This book teaches you that God keeps his promises even when the people who carry those promises fail spectacularly. That's not just David's story. That's the gospel.

BEFORE YOU BEGIN

A word of warning: 2 Samuel contains some of the most difficult material in the Bible. There is violence, some of it graphic. There is sexual sin. There is a devastating assault on a young woman by her own half-brother. There is manipulation, murder, and family betrayal. The book doesn't flinch from any of it.

Why does the Bible include such hard content? Because it tells the truth about what happens when sin is let loose, even in the household of the man after God's own heart. God doesn't sanitize David's story. He shows you the full cost of sin so you'll take it seriously, and he shows you the full reach of grace so you'll never give up hope.

As you read, you'll also notice something important about how 2 Samuel tells its story. In the early chapters, David asks God for direction at every turn. "Shall I go up? Shall I pursue?" And God answers every time. But after chapter 11, those conversations disappear. David stops asking. The silence is deafening. It's the writer's way of showing you what sin does: it doesn't just damage your relationships with people. It disrupts your relationship with God. And yet, even in the silence, God is still working, still keeping his promise, still steering the story toward something greater.

THE STORY BEGINS

So here we are, about to walk through the most important reign in Israel's history. We'll watch a shepherd boy finally take his throne. We'll hear God make a promise that will echo for a thousand years. We'll see a king dance in the streets and weep in the streets. We'll meet warriors who killed giants, a woman who guarded her sons' remains through an endless night, and a crippled man who ate at the king's table because of a promise made to his dead father.

We'll also watch a great man do a terrible thing and spend the rest of his life living with what it cost.

And through it all, behind every triumph and every disaster, we'll see a God who is faithful when his people aren't, who disciplines because he loves, who keeps building his kingdom even when the builders break.

David is not the hero of this story. God is. David is the Christ-shaped, Christ-needing, Christ-pointing king through whom God chose to work, not because David was perfect but because God's grace is.

Turn the page.

1

WHEN YOUR ENEMY FALLS

In Disney's *Robin Hood*, Prince John is a fraud. He's sitting on the throne, wearing the crown, and ordering everyone around, but the real king, Richard, is far away. Prince John didn't earn his power. He grabbed it. And the people around him are even worse. The Sheriff of Nottingham squeezes taxes out of helpless villagers. Sir Hiss whispers schemes into the prince's ear. Everyone in Prince John's circle is trying to gain something through manipulation, intimidation, or brute force.

But Robin Hood operates by a completely different set of rules. He's loyal to the true king. He takes risks not for personal gain but for the good of people who can't defend themselves. When he has opportunities to seize power, he doesn't. He'd rather do the right thing and wait for the rightful king to return.

That contrast, between people who grab for power and people who wait for it to come the right way, is exactly what you're about to see in 2 Samuel 1–4. These chapters are full of people trying to hand David the kingdom through lies, murder, and political scheming. And every single time, David refuses to accept it on those terms. He won't take a throne that's been handed to him at the point of a sword. He'll wait for God.

What makes this even more remarkable is the identity of the man who just died. Saul, the king who spent years trying to kill David, is dead. David's greatest enemy is gone. The road to the throne is wide open. If ever there was a moment to celebrate, this was it.

David didn't celebrate. He wept.

THE LIAR FROM THE BATTLEFIELD

When 2 Samuel opens, David has just returned to the town of Ziklag after rescuing his people from an Amalekite raid. He doesn't know yet what's happened up north on Mount Gilboa. He doesn't know that Saul and Jonathan are dead.

Then a messenger arrives. The man's clothes are torn and there's dirt on his head, the ancient signs of mourning. He falls face-down in front of David. Something terrible has happened.

David asks what's going on, and the man delivers the news: Israel's army has been crushed. Many soldiers are dead. And Saul and Jonathan, Saul's son, are among the fallen.

But then the story takes a strange turn. The messenger, an Amalekite, claims that he personally killed Saul. He says he found Saul leaning on his spear, badly wounded, with the enemy closing in. Saul begged the Amalekite to finish him off, and the Amalekite says he did. As proof, he presents Saul's crown and armband.

Here's the problem: the man is lying.

If you read 1 Samuel 31, you already know what really happened. Saul fell on his own sword. No Amalekite was involved. This man almost certainly found Saul's body after the battle, grabbed the royal insignia, and then made up a heroic story to impress David. He figured David would be thrilled that Saul was dead. He expected a reward. Maybe even a government position.

He figured wrong.

A GRIEF NOBODY EXPECTED

David's reaction stunned everyone. Instead of celebrating, he grabbed his clothes and tore them, the most extreme expression of grief in the ancient world. Every man with him did the same. They wailed. They wept. They fasted until evening. They mourned for Saul, for Jonathan, for the soldiers who had died, for the entire nation of Israel.

Think about that. Saul had hunted David for years. He had thrown spears at David's head. He had chased him through wilderness and desert. He had tried to have him killed over and over again. And now David was on his knees, weeping for him.

This wasn't an act. David genuinely grieved. Not because Saul had been a good king or a good man, but because Saul was the Lord's anointed. God had chosen Saul, and no matter how far Saul had fallen, David never stopped respecting the office God had given him.

After the weeping, David turned back to the Amalekite. "Where are you from?" he asked. The man admitted he was an Amalekite who had been living in Israel. He should have known better.

David's next question was devastating: "Why were you not afraid to lift your hand to destroy the Lord's anointed?"

The Amalekite had no answer. David ordered his execution on the spot. "Your blood is on your own head," David told him. "Your own mouth testified against you."

The man had come expecting a promotion. He left in a coffin. He was punished for the very thing he bragged about, even though he hadn't actually done it. His lie became his death sentence.

THE SONG THAT WOULDN'T LET GO

David didn't just grieve privately. He wrote a song. It's called the Lament of the Bow, and it's one of the most beautiful and heartbreaking poems in the entire Bible. David ordered that it be taught to the men of Judah so they would never forget what happened at Gilboa.

The poem begins with a line that echoes through the whole thing like a drumbeat: "How the mighty have fallen!"

David cursed the mountains of Gilboa, wishing that no dew or rain would ever fall on them again, because that's where Israel's warriors were slaughtered. He begged that the news not be spread in Philistine cities, because he couldn't stand the thought of Israel's enemies celebrating.

Then he turned to Saul and Jonathan specifically. He praised their skill as warriors. He called them "beloved and lovely" and said that "in life and in death they were not divided." Jonathan had stayed loyal to his father all the way to the end, even though he knew David was the one God had chosen to be king. He died fighting beside Saul on that hill. David honored that loyalty.

And then David said something about Jonathan that has echoed for three thousand years: "I am distressed for you, my brother Jonathan; very pleasant have you been to me; your love to me was extraordinary."

This was real grief. Deep, aching, personal grief. David had lost the best friend he would ever have. The man who had risked everything for him, who had given up his own claim to the throne, who had once said, "You will be king over Israel, and I will be second to you." That man was gone.

"How the mighty have fallen," David sang again, "and the weapons of war have perished."

KING OF JUDAH

With Saul dead, David didn't rush to claim the throne. Instead, he did what he had always done: he asked God what to do. "Shall I go up to one of the towns of Judah?" David asked. God answered clearly: "Go up to Hebron."

So David moved his entire household, his two wives, and all his men and their families to Hebron, the most important city in the southern tribe of Judah. There the men of Judah anointed David as king over their tribe.

It was a real moment. After years of running, hiding, and waiting, David was finally a king. But it was a small kingdom. One tribe. A few hill towns in the south. David ruled from Hebron while the rest of Israel followed someone else entirely.

That someone was Ish-bosheth, a surviving son of Saul. But Ish-bosheth wasn't really in charge. He was a puppet. The real power behind the northern kingdom was Abner, the commander of Saul's army. Abner had taken Ish-bosheth across the Jordan River to a town called Mahanaim and set him up as king over the northern tribes. It was a political move, not a spiritual one. Abner wanted to keep power in his own hands, and a weak king was the perfect tool for that.

So Israel was divided. David in the south. Ish-bosheth in the north. And between them, a long and bitter civil war.

A WAR NOBODY WON

The conflict between the two kingdoms was brutal. Early on, the two armies met at the pool of Gibeon. Abner, commanding Ish-bosheth's forces, and Joab, David's general, sat on opposite sides of the pool and agreed to a contest: twelve warriors from each side would fight. All twenty-four died. Then a full-scale battle erupted.

David's men won that day, but the victory came at a personal cost. Joab had a younger brother named Asahel, who was incredibly fast, "as swift as a wild gazelle." Asahel chased Abner across the battlefield. Abner warned him twice to stop. "Turn aside," Abner said. "Why should I strike you down? How could I look your brother Joab in the face?" But Asahel wouldn't quit. Abner killed him with a single backward thrust of his spear.

That death planted a seed of revenge in Joab's heart that would bear terrible fruit later. Remember that. It matters.

The summary of this period is simple but powerful: "The war between the house of Saul and the house of David lasted a long time. David grew stronger and stronger, while the house of Saul grew weaker and weaker."

God's chosen king was rising. The rival kingdom was fading. But the path between the two was soaked in blood.

ABNER SWITCHES SIDES

Eventually, Abner, the real power in the north, had a falling-out with Ish-bosheth. After a heated argument over one of Saul's former wives, Abner decided he was done propping up a failing dynasty. He sent messengers to David with an offer: "I'll bring all of Israel over to you."

David agreed, but he had one condition. He wanted Michal, Saul's daughter and David's first wife, returned to him. (Saul had taken her away years earlier and given her to another man.) The request was political as well as personal. Having Saul's daughter back at his side would strengthen David's claim to the throne in the eyes of the northern tribes.

Abner delivered. He spoke with the elders of Israel and the leaders of Benjamin, Saul's own tribe. He told them what they already suspected: "For some time you have wanted to make David your king. Now do it!" He came to Hebron, met with David, shared a meal, and left in peace with a plan to unite the entire nation under David's rule.

It was the closest Israel had been to reunification since Saul's death.

Then Joab ruined everything.

MURDER AT THE GATE

Joab returned from a raid to discover that Abner had been in Hebron and David had sent him away in peace. Joab was furious. He sent messengers to bring Abner back, without David's knowledge. When Abner arrived at the gate of Hebron, Joab pulled him aside as if to speak privately and stabbed him in the stomach. Abner died on the spot.

Joab claimed it was payback for his brother Asahel's death. But the Bible calls it what it was: murder. Abner had killed Asahel in battle, in self-defense, after warning him twice. Joab killed Abner in peacetime, by deception, at the gate of a city of refuge where violence was supposed to be forbidden.

David was devastated. He publicly cursed Joab and his family. He ordered everyone to mourn for Abner. He walked behind the coffin himself and wept at the grave. He refused to eat for the rest of the day. And he composed another lament: "Should Abner have died as the lawless die? Your hands were not bound, your feet were not fettered. You fell as one falls before wicked men."

The people noticed. They saw David's grief was real. And the text says that "all the people and all Israel knew that the king had no part in the murder of Abner."

David told his men the truth: "These sons of Zeruiah are too strong for me." Joab was David's own nephew and his best general. David couldn't simply execute him without risking civil war within his own ranks. But he refused to pretend what Joab did was acceptable. He left Joab's judgment to God.

THE HEAD ON THE FLOOR

With Abner dead, the northern kingdom collapsed. Ish-bosheth "lost heart," and all of Israel was terrified. Without Abner, the puppet had no one pulling his strings.

Two of Ish-bosheth's own military officers, brothers named Rechab and Baanah, decided to seize the moment. They snuck into Ish-bosheth's house during his afternoon nap, stabbed him in the stomach, cut off his head, and traveled all night to deliver it to David at Hebron.

They were proud of themselves. They presented the head to David and said, "Here is the head of Ish-bosheth son of Saul, your enemy, who tried to take your life. This day the Lord has avenged my lord the king against Saul and his offspring."

Did you catch that? They wrapped their murder in theology. They claimed God was behind it. They expected David to thank them.

David's response was ice-cold. He reminded them of what he'd done to the last person who brought him "good news" about Saul's death. "I seized him and put him to death in Ziklag," David said. "That was the reward I gave him for his news."

Then David said something that reveals the deepest truth about his character. He took an oath: "As the Lord lives, who has redeemed my life out of every adversity." That's the key. David knew that his safety, his survival, and his path to the throne didn't depend on murderers doing favors for him. It depended entirely on God. God was the one who had rescued him from every danger. God was the one who would bring him to the throne. David didn't need the help of wicked men, and he certainly wasn't going to reward them for it.

Rechab and Baanah were executed. Their bodies were hung by the pool in Hebron as a warning. Ish-bosheth's head was buried with honor in Abner's tomb.

WHAT THIS MEANS FOR US

First, the right thing gained the wrong way is still wrong. The Amalekite, Rechab, and Baanah all tried to help David by doing terrible things. They assumed the end justified the means. David rejected that logic every time. If God has promised you something, you don't need to lie, cheat, or hurt people to get it. If you have to sin to reach your goal, the goal isn't worth reaching.

Second, grief can be an act of faith. David grieved for an enemy. He didn't pretend Saul had been a great king or ignore the years of pain Saul had caused him. But he honored the office Saul held and the God who had placed him there. When someone falls, even someone who hurt you, it's possible to grieve without approving of everything they did. That kind of grief takes real maturity.

Third, God's timing is better than your impatience. David could have marched north and taken the whole kingdom by force. He had the military strength to do it. Instead, he waited. He asked God before making each move. He let the rival kingdom collapse on its own. It took more than seven years, but David trusted that the God who had promised him the throne would deliver it in his own time.

Fourth, don't let people use God's name to justify evil. Rechab and Baanah claimed God was behind their murder. They dressed up their sin in religious language. David saw right through it. People still do this today. They use the Bible, prayer, or spiritual language to cover up selfish, hurtful, or dishonest behavior. Real faith shows up in how you treat people, not in how you talk about God while mistreating them.

Fifth, gratitude protects you from temptation. When Rechab and Baanah showed up, David could have been tempted to accept their gift. After all, Ish-bosheth's death did clear his path to the throne. But David remembered who had truly protected him: "The Lord, who has redeemed my life out of every adversity." When you remember what God has already done for you, it's much harder to be tricked into crediting evil men for God's blessings.

TALKING POINTS

1. **David mourned deeply for Saul, even though Saul had been his enemy for years.** Why do you think David was able to grieve for someone who had tried to kill him? What does this teach us about how we should respond when something bad happens to someone who has hurt us?

2. **The Amalekite and later Rechab and Baanah all expected David to reward them for removing his rivals.** Why do you think people assume that the "winner" will be happy to hear about the downfall of their opponent? What does David's response tell us about his character?

3. **David asked God for direction before moving to Hebron, even though it probably seemed obvious that he should go there.** Why is it important to seek God's guidance even when the right move seems clear? How can we practice this in our own decisions?

4. **Rechab and Baanah used religious language to justify their murder, saying God had "avenged" David.** Have you ever seen someone use God or the Bible to excuse bad behavior? How can we tell the difference between someone genuinely following God and someone just using God's name?

5. **David said God had "redeemed my life out of every adversity."** What does it mean to trust that God is the one protecting and guiding your life? How might remembering past moments when God helped you make it easier to trust him with what's ahead?

David had been king of Judah for more than seven years. In that time, he had buried his best friend, mourned his worst enemy, refused rewards from murderers, and watched a rival kingdom crumble without lifting a sword against it. He hadn't grabbed a single thing. He had waited. He had trusted. He had grieved when others expected him to celebrate and punished when others expected him to reward.

Now, with Ish-bosheth dead and the northern tribes leaderless, Israel was about to come looking for a king. And they already knew who it should be.

Turn the page.

2

A SEAT AT THE TABLE

In Disney's *The Sword in the Stone*, a scrawny orphan named Arthur does everything wrong. He's clumsy. He's small. Everyone calls him Wart. He works as a servant in a castle that isn't his, polishing armor for a knight who barely notices he exists. Arthur has no title, no family name, and no reason to expect anything from life except more chores and more invisibility.

When every knight and nobleman in England lines up to pull the legendary sword from the stone, nobody even thinks to invite Arthur. He only touches it because he needs a replacement sword for his master and grabs the nearest one without realizing what it is. He pulls it free without effort, and suddenly the boy nobody noticed is the King of England.

Arthur didn't campaign for the throne. He didn't fight for it. He didn't even understand what was happening. The crown simply came to him because it was always meant to be his.

That feeling, of receiving something so enormous you can barely understand it, runs through every page of 2 Samuel 5–9. A shepherd boy who spent years hiding in caves finally receives a throne. A king who wants to build God a temple is told that God is going to build *him* a dynasty instead. And a crippled grandson of David's dead enemy, hiding in a forgotten village, expecting nothing but punishment, is summoned to the palace and given a permanent place at the king's table.

Nobody in these chapters earns what they receive. That's the point. From the throne room to the dinner table, this section of 2 Samuel is about a God who gives people more than they could ever ask for, more than they could ever deserve, and more than they could ever imagine.

THE SHEPHERD TAKES THE THRONE

After more than seven years as king of only Judah, the rest of Israel finally came to David. The northern tribes arrived at Hebron and made their case: "We're your flesh and blood. Even when Saul was king, you were the one actually leading us in battle. And the Lord said you would shepherd his people Israel."

That last argument was the one that mattered most. God had promised David the throne. The elders knew it. The tribes knew it. And now, at last, they were ready to acknowledge it. David made a covenant with them, and they anointed him king over all Israel. He was thirty years old, and he would reign for forty years.

The promise God had made to a teenage shepherd back in Bethlehem, the promise that had survived Saul's spears, years of running through the wilderness, and a brutal civil war, had finally come true.

David's first major act as king was brilliant. He marched to Jerusalem, a fortress city controlled by the Jebusites, a people who had never been conquered. The Jebusites were so confident in their walls that they taunted David: "Even the blind and the lame can keep you out."

David took the city anyway.

Jerusalem was a strategic masterpiece as a capital. It sat on the border between the northern and southern tribes, belonging to neither, making it a neutral site that could unite the whole nation. David renamed it the City of David and began building it up. The text gives us the reason for his success in a single sentence: "And David became greater and greater, for the Lord, the God of hosts, was with him."

THE DAY EVERYTHING WENT WRONG

With a new capital and a united kingdom, David turned his attention to the most important symbol of God's presence: the ark of the covenant. The ark had been sitting in a private home in an obscure village ever since the Philistines captured and returned it decades earlier. Saul had basically ignored it for his entire reign. David wanted to bring it to Jerusalem, right to the heart of his new capital, where God's presence would be at the center of the nation's life.

It was a great idea. The execution was a disaster.

David assembled thirty thousand men and loaded the ark onto a brand-new cart pulled by oxen. The whole nation celebrated with music and singing as the procession moved toward Jerusalem. Then the oxen stumbled. A man named Uzzah reached out to steady the ark, and God struck him dead on the spot.

The celebration stopped. The music stopped. Everyone stood in stunned silence.

David was angry. Then he was afraid. "How can the ark of the Lord ever come to me?" he asked. He left the ark at the house of a man named Obed-edom and went home.

This is a hard passage. Uzzah seemed to be doing a good thing. He was trying to keep the ark from falling. But God had given specific instructions in the Law about how the ark was supposed to be transported: carried by Levites using poles, never touched by human hands. David had ignored those instructions and put the ark on a cart instead, copying the way the Philistines had transported it. The whole operation, however well-meaning, was careless with God's holiness.

The lesson was painful but important: God's presence is a gift, not a convenience. You don't approach a holy God on your own terms, no matter how good your intentions are.

Three months later, after hearing that God had blessed Obed-edom's household because of the ark, David tried again. This time he did it right. The Levites carried the ark on their shoulders as God had commanded. Every six steps, they stopped to offer sacrifices. And David himself danced before the Lord "with all his might," wearing a simple linen garment instead of his royal robes. The king of Israel was leaping and spinning in the streets like a child, and he didn't care who was watching.

When the ark finally entered Jerusalem, the people shouted and the trumpets blew. God's presence was home.

Not everyone was impressed. Michal, David's wife and Saul's daughter, watched from a window and despised David for what she considered undignified behavior. When David came home, she mocked him. David's answer was sharp: "It was before the Lord, who chose me rather than your father. I will celebrate before the Lord." Michal's contempt for David's worship left her childless for the rest of her life.

The contrast between David and Michal is the contrast between two ways of approaching God: wholehearted abandon or cold, calculated pride. David chose abandon. It cost him dignity. It gained him joy.

THE PROMISE THAT CHANGED EVERYTHING

With the ark settled in Jerusalem, David was sitting in his new cedar palace one evening when a thought struck him. He was living in a beautiful house, but God's ark was still sitting in a tent. That didn't seem right. He told the prophet Nathan his plan: he wanted to build God a proper temple, a permanent house.

Nathan's first response was encouraging: "Go ahead. The Lord is with you."

But that night, God gave Nathan a different message. And it turned out to be one of the most important revelations in the entire Bible.

God told Nathan to go back to David and say this: "Are you the one to build me a house? I've never asked for a house of cedar. I've been traveling in a tent with my people since I brought them out of Egypt, and I've never complained about it." God wasn't offended by David's offer. He was redirecting it.

Then came the twist. God said, in effect, "You're not going to build me a house. I'm going to build you one."

But "house" didn't mean a building. It meant a dynasty, a family line. And the promise God made to David that night is staggering:

God would raise up David's son after him and establish his kingdom. That son would build the temple David dreamed of. God would be a father to him, and he would be a son to God. If he sinned, God would discipline him, but God would never take his love away the way he took it from Saul. And here's the climax: "Your house and your kingdom shall be made sure forever before me. Your throne shall be established forever."

Forever. David's throne would last forever.

This promise, sometimes called the Davidic Covenant, is one of the most important promises in the entire Bible. It's the reason the prophets kept looking for a future king from David's line. It's the reason the angel told Mary that her son would sit on "the throne of his father David" and that "his kingdom will never end." It's the reason Matthew starts his Gospel by calling Jesus "the son of David." Everything about the coming of Jesus is rooted in the promise God made to David that night.

David's response was pure worship. He sat before the Lord and prayed one of the most beautiful prayers in Scripture. "Who am I, O Lord God, and what is my house, that you have brought me this far?" He didn't argue or ask for more. He simply marveled at the grace of a God who gives more than anyone could ask or imagine.

"Do as you have promised," David prayed. That's all he could say. God's promise was already more than enough.

THE KINGDOM EXPANDS

Chapter 8 reads like a highlight reel. David defeated the Philistines, the Moabites, the king of Zobah, the Arameans, and the Edomites. His kingdom stretched from the borders of Egypt to the Euphrates River. The chapter keeps repeating one phrase like a drumbeat: "The Lord gave David victory wherever he went."

This wasn't David being a military genius. This was God keeping his promise. He had told David he would give him rest from all his enemies, and now he was doing exactly that. David's victories fulfilled not only the promise of 2 Samuel 7 but reached all the way back to the promise God made to Abraham in Genesis 15, that his descendants would possess this land. Eight hundred years later, under David, it was finally happening.

The chapter closes with a summary of David's government: "David reigned over all Israel, and David administered justice and equity to all his people." This is what a kingdom looks like when its king follows God. Justice for everyone. Peace on every border. A nation thriving under the rule of the Lord's anointed.

THE CRIPPLE AT THE KING'S TABLE

Then David asked a question that nobody expected: "Is there anyone still left of the house of Saul to whom I can show kindness for Jonathan's sake?"

In the ancient world, when a new king took the throne, the standard practice was to wipe out every surviving member of the previous dynasty. You didn't leave potential rivals alive. It was Politics 101: solidify your power by eliminating the competition.

David didn't want to eliminate anyone. He wanted to bless them.

A servant named Ziba told David there was one survivor: a son of Jonathan named Mephibosheth. He was living in a remote place called Lo-debar, and he was crippled in both feet. When he was five years old, news had arrived that Saul and Jonathan were dead. His nurse grabbed him and fled in panic, and in the chaos he was dropped. He'd been lame ever since.

David sent for him. When Mephibosheth arrived, he fell on his face before the king. He was terrified. He knew what happened to the grandsons of fallen kings. He probably expected to die.

David said three words that changed everything: "Do not fear."

Then he piled on more grace than Mephibosheth could have dreamed of. He restored all of Saul's land to him. He assigned Ziba and his household to manage the estate on Mephibosheth's behalf. And then he gave him the greatest honor of all: "You shall eat at my table always."

Mephibosheth was stunned. "What is your servant," he said, "that you should show regard for a dead dog such as I?"

From that day forward, Jonathan's crippled son ate at the king's table like one of David's own children. The last line of the chapter is devastating in its simplicity: "So Mephibosheth lived in Jerusalem, for he ate always at the king's table. And he was lame in both his feet."

Lame in both feet. But seated at the king's table. That's grace.

David showed kindness to Mephibosheth because of a promise he had made to Jonathan years earlier. But the echoes run much deeper. A helpless person. An enemy's descendant. Summoned from a far-off place. Given an inheritance he didn't earn. Seated at the king's table forever. If that doesn't sound like the gospel, read it again.

WHAT THIS MEANS FOR US

First, God keeps his promises, even when it takes centuries. The promise to Abraham about the land was eight hundred years old when David conquered the Jebusites. The promise to David about an eternal throne wouldn't find its ultimate fulfillment until Jesus was born a thousand years later. God is not in a hurry, but he is never late. If he has promised something, it will happen.

Second, good intentions don't replace obedience. David meant well when he put the ark on a cart. His heart was in the right place. But God had already told his people how the ark was to be carried. Good intentions are important, but they don't override God's instructions. How we worship matters, not just that we worship.

Third, God gives more than we could ask for. David wanted to give God a temple. God gave David an eternal dynasty. David's generosity was real, but God's generosity was infinitely greater. That's how God works. You come with your small offering, and he comes back with something so enormous you can barely take it in.

Fourth, grace goes to the most unlikely people. Mephibosheth was crippled, afraid, and the grandson of David's enemy. He had nothing to offer. He was living in a forgotten place. And David sought him out, not to punish him but to bless him. If God can seat a broken enemy at his table, he can do the same for you.

Fifth, the whole story points to Jesus. David's throne, David's covenant, David's kindness, it all casts a long shadow forward. Jesus is the son of David who reigns forever. Jesus is the one who seeks out the broken and the lost and invites them to his table. The promise God made in 2 Samuel 7 is the promise that Christ fulfills.

TALKING POINTS

1. **David waited more than seven years to become king of all Israel.** What does his patience teach us about trusting God's timing, especially when a promise seems to be taking too long?
2. **The death of Uzzah feels harsh to modern readers.** Why do you think God responded so strongly? What does this teach us about how we approach God, even when we mean well?
3. **David danced before the Lord with "all his might," and Michal despised him for it.** What's the difference between worshiping to impress people and worshiping because you can't contain your joy? Which one do you lean toward?
4. **When David wanted to build God a house, God said, "Let me build you one instead."** Have you ever made plans for God only to discover that God had bigger plans for you? What happened?
5. **David invited Mephibosheth to his table even though Mephibosheth was the grandson of his enemy.** How does this story help you understand what it means for God to show grace to people who don't deserve it, including you?

The shepherd boy who once played his harp in a Bethlehem pasture was now the king of a united nation, ruling from a fortified capital, with God's ark at the center of his city and God's promise anchoring his future. Everything David had hoped for and more had come to pass. God had built him a house no storm could topple.

But a storm was coming anyway. And it wouldn't come from the Philistines or the Moabites or any foreign army. It would come from inside David's own heart.

Turn the page.

3

WHEN THE HERO FALLS

In Oscar Wilde's *The Picture of Dorian Gray*, a young man named Dorian has his portrait painted by a talented artist. Through strange circumstances, something impossible happens: Dorian stays young and handsome no matter what he does, but the painting changes. Every selfish act, every cruel choice, every hidden sin shows up on the canvas instead of on his face. While Dorian looks perfect to the world, the portrait locked away in his attic reveals what he's really becoming. Over time, the painting grows so twisted and ugly that Dorian can barely stand to look at it. But he keeps the attic door locked. As long as nobody sees the painting, he thinks, nobody has to know.

That story haunts me when I read 2 Samuel 11.

Up to this point, David has been the hero of the story. The brave shepherd. The giant-killer. The man after God's own heart. The king who danced before the Lord. The ruler who showed kindness to a crippled enemy. If anyone in the Bible seemed beyond a catastrophic moral failure, it was David.

But every human heart has an attic. And in one terrible season, David locked something in his that would change everything. He sinned. He lied. He destroyed an innocent man's life. And for months, he walked around looking like the same righteous king while the portrait behind the locked door grew darker and darker.

Until God sent someone to kick the door open.

THE WAR THAT STARTED IT ALL

Before we get to David's fall, we need to understand the background. Chapter 10 tells us that the king of the Ammonites died and his son Hanun took the throne. David, remembering a kindness Hanun's father had once shown him, sent diplomats to express his sympathy. It was a classy move, the kind of gracious act we'd expect from David.

Hanun's advisors convinced him it was a trick. They told the young king that David's men were really spies. So Hanun humiliated David's ambassadors by shaving off half their beards and cutting their robes short, then sent them home in disgrace.

It was an act of stunning foolishness. The Ammonites knew they'd made an enemy of the most powerful king in the region, so they hired mercenary armies from the north to help them fight. It didn't work. Joab, David's general, defeated both the Ammonites and their hired soldiers. A second, even larger coalition came against Israel and was crushed. David's enemies made peace and submitted to his rule.

The war with Ammon wasn't fully over, though. Rabbah, the Ammonite capital, still needed to be taken. As the next fighting season began, David sent Joab and the army to finish the job.

But David stayed home.

THE MOMENT EVERYTHING CHANGED

That single sentence, "But David remained at Jerusalem," is one of the most ominous lines in the Bible. It's the time of year when kings go out to battle, and David is on the roof of his palace with nothing to do.

Late one afternoon, David got up from a nap and was walking on his rooftop when he noticed a woman bathing in a nearby courtyard. She was very beautiful. David asked his servants who she was. The answer came back loaded with warnings: "Is not this Bathsheba, the daughter of Eliam, the wife of Uriah the Hittite?"

She was married. Her husband was one of David's own elite soldiers, a brave and loyal warrior who was away risking his life in the very war David had stayed home from.

None of that stopped David. He sent for Bathsheba, and he slept with her. The man who had shown such self-control in the wilderness, who had twice refused to kill Saul when he had the chance, who had waited years for God's timing, threw it all away in a single evening.

This is one of the hardest parts of the Bible to read. Not because it's confusing, but because it's David. If David can fall this hard, what does that say about the rest of us?

THE COVER-UP

A short time later, Bathsheba sent David a two-word message: "I'm pregnant."

This was a crisis. Her husband had been away at war. If anyone found out, the consequences under the law would be severe for both of them. David could have confessed. He could have come clean, faced the fallout, and thrown himself on God's mercy. Instead, he chose to cover it up. And the cover-up was worse than the crime.

David summoned Uriah home from the battlefield. He pretended he wanted a report on the war, asked casual questions about how things were going, and then told Uriah to go home and relax with his wife. David's plan was simple: if Uriah spent the night at home, everyone would assume the child was his.

But Uriah refused to go home. While his fellow soldiers were sleeping in open fields and the ark of God was housed in a tent on the front lines, Uriah said he could not in good conscience enjoy the comforts of his own bed. He slept with the palace guards instead.

Think about the irony. The foreign-born soldier showed more honor and faithfulness than the king of Israel. Uriah wouldn't even go home to his wife out of loyalty to his comrades and his God. David, meanwhile, had already betrayed both.

David tried again the next night, inviting Uriah to dinner and getting him drunk. Surely this would lower his defenses. It didn't. Even drunk, Uriah's sense of duty held. He slept with the guards again.

David was running out of options. And rather than stop and turn back, he went deeper.

THE LETTER

The next morning David wrote a letter to Joab, his general, and he sent it to the front lines in Uriah's own hand. Uriah carried his own death warrant and didn't know it.

The letter said: "Put Uriah at the front where the fighting is fiercest. Then pull back from him so that he will be struck down and killed."

Read that again. The king of Israel, God's anointed, the man who wrote psalms about the Lord's faithfulness, ordered the murder of an innocent man to hide his own sin. This wasn't a moment of weakness. This was a calculated, cold-blooded plan.

Joab obeyed. He placed Uriah in a dangerous position during the next assault on the city. Uriah fought bravely, as he always did. And he died, along with several other soldiers who were caught in the same deadly maneuver.

When the report came back to David that Uriah was dead, the king's response was chilling in its casualness: "Don't let this upset you. The sword devours one as well as another." He said it as though Uriah's death were just an unfortunate casualty of war. As though he hadn't ordered it himself.

After Bathsheba mourned her husband, David brought her to the palace and married her. She had a son. From the outside, everything looked tidy. The crisis was handled. The secret was safe.

Then the narrator drops a single devastating sentence: "But the thing David had done displeased the Lord."

God had been watching the whole time.

YOU ARE THE MAN

"And the Lord sent Nathan to David." Those seven words are among the most important in the Bible. God didn't abandon David. He didn't let his servant rot in hidden sin. He sent a prophet to drag the truth into the light. That's not punishment. That's grace, even though it wouldn't feel like it.

Nathan didn't charge in shouting accusations. He was smarter than that. He told David a story.

"There were two men in a certain city," Nathan began. "One was rich and one was poor. The rich man had enormous flocks and herds, more than he could count. The poor man had nothing except one little lamb. He raised it by hand. It grew up with his children, ate from his plate, drank from his cup, slept in his arms. It was like a daughter to him.

"Then a traveler came to visit the rich man. But instead of taking one of his own sheep to feed his guest, the rich man took the poor man's only lamb and killed it."

David exploded. He swore an oath: "As the Lord lives, the man who did this deserves to die! He must repay four times over because he did this thing and had no pity."

Nathan looked at the king and said four words that split David's world in half:

"You are the man."

Then Nathan delivered God's message. God reminded David of everything he'd been given: the throne, Saul's kingdom, safety from his enemies, more than he could ever need. "If that were too little," God said, "I would have given you even more. Why have you despised the word of the Lord by doing what is evil in his sight?"

The consequences would be severe. Violence would haunt David's family from that day forward. The sword would not depart from his house. What David had done in secret would come back to him in public. The child Bathsheba was carrying would die.

THREE WORDS

Here is where David and Saul part ways forever. When Saul was confronted with his sin, he made excuses. He blamed the soldiers. He rationalized. He argued. He admitted guilt only when cornered and then immediately begged Samuel not to embarrass him in front of the people. Saul's confession was about managing his reputation.

David's confession was three words: "I have sinned."

No excuses. No deflection. No "but you don't understand the pressure I was under." No blaming Bathsheba or Joab or the situation. Just the raw, simple truth: "I have sinned against the Lord."

Nathan's response was immediate: "The Lord has put away your sin. You will not die."

That's grace. David deserved death under the law. He received forgiveness instead. Not because he earned it. Not because his confession was impressive enough. But because God is the kind of God who forgives when we come to him honestly.

But forgiveness didn't erase the consequences. The child became ill and died, just as Nathan had said. David fasted and prayed desperately while the baby was sick, hoping God would show mercy. When the child died, David's servants were afraid to tell him. They thought he might harm himself.

David surprised everyone. He got up, washed his face, changed his clothes, and went to worship God. Then he came home and ate. His servants were confused. Why had he fasted while the child was alive but stopped after the child died?

David's answer revealed something deep about his understanding of God: "While the child was still alive, I fasted and wept. I thought, 'Who knows? The Lord may be gracious to me and let the child live.' But now he is dead. Why should I fast? Can I bring him back? I will go to him, but he will not return to me."

David grieved. But he didn't despair. He knew God's character well enough to hope during the crisis, and he trusted God's purposes well enough to accept the outcome. That's not cold indifference. That's faith forged in the furnace of consequences.

SOMETHING NEW FROM SOMETHING BROKEN

Sometime later, David and Bathsheba had another son. They named him Solomon. And the text adds a line that still catches me off guard every time I read it: "And the Lord loved him."

Out of David's worst failure, God was already building something new. Solomon would become the wisest king in Israel's history. He would build the temple David had dreamed of. He would sit on the throne God had promised would last forever. The child born from this broken, painful, redeemed story would carry the promise forward.

That doesn't mean the sin didn't matter. It mattered enormously. David's family would never be the same. The consequences Nathan described would unfold in agonizing detail over the next several chapters. But God's ability to bring life out of wreckage is one of the most persistent themes in the entire Bible. He doesn't approve of the wreckage. He redeems it.

The chapter closes by returning to the war. Joab captured most of Rabbah and summoned David to deliver the final blow. David came, took the city, and the Ammonite conflict was finally over.

But the real battle, the one inside David's heart, was only beginning.

WHAT THIS MEANS FOR US

First, no one is above falling. David wasn't a bad person. He was one of the greatest men of faith in the Bible. But in a moment of idleness, when he was in the wrong place at the wrong time with the wrong thoughts, he made a choice that wrecked lives. If David can fall, so can anyone. The moment you think you're safe from temptation is the moment you're most vulnerable.

Second, small compromises lead to catastrophic ones. David didn't wake up one morning and decide to destroy an innocent man. He stayed home when he should have been leading. He looked when he should have turned away. He inquired when he should have stopped. He sent for her when he should have walked back inside. Each step was small. Together they were devastating. Sin almost never announces itself. It whispers, one step at a time.

Third, God sees what no one else sees. For months, David thought he had gotten away with it. The secret was buried. The story was clean. But the narrator waited until the very last line to remind us: "The thing David had done displeased the Lord." God's silence is not God's absence. He sees behind every locked door.

Fourth, how you respond to correction reveals your heart. The difference between David and Saul wasn't that David sinned less. It was that David, when confronted, didn't make excuses. He confessed. He broke. He submitted. The measure of a person's character is not whether they fail but what they do when their failure is exposed.

Fifth, God's grace is greater than your worst sin. David committed adultery and murder. He received forgiveness. That doesn't minimize what he did. It magnifies who God is. If you've done something you think God could never forgive, David's story says otherwise. But grace always calls for honesty first. You can't receive what you won't admit you need.

TALKING POINTS

1. **David stayed home when he should have been with his army.** How can boredom, idleness, or being in the wrong place make us more vulnerable to bad choices? What safeguards can we build into our lives?

2. **David's sin started with a look and escalated into adultery, deception, and murder.** Why is it so hard to stop a chain of bad decisions once it starts? What would it have looked like for David to stop at each stage?

3. **Uriah, the foreign-born soldier, showed more integrity than the king of Israel.** What does his example teach us about faithfulness, especially when no one would notice if we cut corners?

4. **When Nathan confronted David, David said simply, "I have sinned." Compare this to how Saul responded when confronted in 1 Samuel 15.** What's the difference between real repentance and just trying to avoid consequences?

5. **God forgave David, but the consequences of his sin remained.** Why do you think God works this way? How does understanding that forgiveness doesn't erase consequences change the way you think about your own choices?

The king who danced before the Lord had fallen harder than anyone thought possible. His sin would echo through his family for generations. Sons would rebel. A kingdom would fracture. Blood would be spilled in David's own household, just as Nathan had warned.

But David was still on the throne. Still God's chosen king. Still forgiven. And from the ashes of his worst failure, a child named Solomon was growing up, loved by the Lord, carrying a promise that nothing, not even the king's darkest hour, could destroy.

The consequences, however, were already on their way.

Turn the page.

4

THE FIRE INSIDE THE HOUSE

In Disney's *The Rescuers*, a little orphan girl named Penny is kidnapped by the villainous Madame Medusa and taken to a remote bayou. Medusa forces Penny into a flooded cave again and again to search for a priceless diamond, because Penny is small enough to fit through the opening. Penny begs for help. She writes letters and stuffs them into bottles, sending them floating down the river, hoping someone, anyone, will read one and come to save her. Nobody does, at least not at first. The adults who should have been looking after her are far away. The authorities who should have noticed she was gone seem oblivious. And Penny is left alone in the hands of someone who only sees her as a tool to get what they want.

What makes the movie work is that eventually two tiny, unlikely heroes, a pair of mice named Bernard and Bianca, do come to rescue Penny. It's a story about the vulnerable being saved.

But not every story ends that way.

In 2 Samuel 13, a young woman named Tamar, the daughter of King David, is trapped by someone more powerful than her. She cries out. She begs. She uses every argument she can think of to stop what's about to happen. And when it's over, she runs through the streets weeping, her robe torn, ashes on her head. The person who should have been her protector, her father, the most powerful man in the nation, hears about everything that happened.

And he does nothing.

No rescue comes. No justice is served. And the consequences of that failure will tear David's family apart.

NATHAN'S PROPHECY COMES TRUE

Before we walk into this chapter, we need to remember something. When Nathan confronted David about his sin with Bathsheba and the murder of Uriah, God's judgment included this: "The sword will not depart from your house." And: "I am raising up trouble against you from your own house."

Up to this point, David's enemies had come from outside. Philistines, Ammonites, the house of Saul. Now the threat was coming from inside his own family. What happens in 2 Samuel 13–14 is the beginning of that terrible prophecy being fulfilled. The violence David inflicted on Uriah's family now echoes inside his own.

This is one of the hardest sections in the entire Bible. But the writer wants you to read it, because it shows you the truth about sin's consequences. Sin doesn't stay contained. It spreads. It infects. It destroys people who had nothing to do with the original choice.

WHAT AMNON DID

David had many sons by different wives. Amnon was the oldest, the heir to the throne. Absalom was another, and Absalom had a sister named Tamar. She was beautiful, and she was a princess.

Amnon became obsessed with Tamar. The text says he was so consumed by what he wanted that he made himself sick over it. He had a friend named Jonadab, David's nephew, who was described as "very crafty." Jonadab noticed Amnon's misery and came up with a plan: pretend to be ill, ask King David to send Tamar over to cook for you, and get her alone.

It worked. David, suspecting nothing, sent Tamar to Amnon's house. She came willingly, prepared food for her half-brother, and brought it to him. Then Amnon sent all his servants out of the room, grabbed Tamar, and told her what he wanted.

Tamar fought back. She begged him to stop. She told him this was wrong, that this kind of thing "is not done in Israel," that it would ruin her life and destroy his reputation. She used every argument she could think of.

Amnon didn't listen. He was stronger than she was, and he attacked her.

What Amnon did to Tamar was an act of terrible violence. He used his power to harm someone who trusted him, someone who had come to his house to help him because their father had asked her to. It was a betrayal of everything a brother, a prince, and a human being was supposed to be.

And then, in one of the most chilling lines in the Bible, Amnon's feelings flipped completely. The obsession he had called "love" turned instantly to hatred. "Get up," he told Tamar. "Get out." He called his servant and ordered him to throw her out and lock the door behind her.

Tamar tore her royal robe, put ashes on her head, and walked away crying out loud for everyone to hear. She went to her brother Absalom's house. The text describes her future in a single devastating word: "desolate." She lived the rest of her days as a broken woman in her brother's household, her life shattered by something she never asked for and couldn't prevent.

THE KING WHO DID NOTHING

Now here is where the story goes from terrible to tragic. "When King David heard of all these things, he was very angry."

Good. He should have been. David was both Tamar's father and the king of Israel. He had the authority and the responsibility to bring Amnon to justice. The law was clear about what Amnon had done. David had every reason and every right to act.

But he didn't. He was furious, and that was all. No punishment. No trial. No protection for Tamar. No public acknowledgment that what Amnon did was wrong.

Why? Many readers have pointed out that David was trapped by his own past. How could he judge Amnon for taking a woman who wasn't his when David himself had done the same thing with Bathsheba? How could he punish his son for abusing power when he had abused his own power as king? David's guilt silenced him. His failure with Bathsheba had stripped him of the moral authority to act, even when acting was exactly what justice demanded.

But understanding David's paralysis doesn't excuse it. He was still the king. He was still her father. Tamar needed someone to stand up for her, and the one person with the power to do it sat on his throne and did nothing.

And when the person responsible for justice refuses to act, someone else usually steps in. That someone was Absalom. And his version of justice would make everything worse.

TWO YEARS OF SILENCE

Absalom said nothing. For two full years after what happened to his sister, Absalom didn't speak to Amnon at all, "neither good nor bad." He didn't confront him. He didn't explode. He didn't go to David demanding action. He just waited.

That silence was not peace. It was a slow-burning fuse.

After two years, Absalom invited all of David's sons to a sheep-shearing festival at his estate in Baal-hazor, about fifteen miles north of Jerusalem. He specifically asked David's permission for Amnon to attend. David was reluctant at first, but Absalom pressed until David agreed.

At the feast, Absalom waited until Amnon was relaxed and drinking. Then he gave the signal. His servants attacked Amnon and killed him. The other princes panicked and fled on their mules back toward Jerusalem.

The first report that reached David was a nightmare: someone told him that Absalom had killed all of the king's sons. David tore his robes and threw himself on the ground. His servants did the same. But Jonadab, the same clever friend who had helped Amnon in the first place, assured David that only Amnon was dead. Jonadab had seen this coming for two years. "This has been Absalom's plan since the day Amnon violated his sister Tamar," he said.

Jonadab was right. And there's something deeply uncomfortable about the fact that the man who helped set the whole disaster in motion was also the one cool enough to explain it when the consequences arrived.

THE EXILE

Absalom fled. He crossed the border and went to Geshur, where his mother's father was king. He stayed there for three years.

David mourned. He mourned for Amnon, who was dead. He mourned over Absalom, who was gone. The text says that over time David's anger toward Absalom faded. He was "spent" from the whole ordeal. But he didn't send for Absalom. He didn't bring him home. He didn't do anything. Once again, David's pattern was clear: anger without action, feelings without follow-through.

Meanwhile, Tamar was still desolate. Nobody asked about her. Nobody restored her. The person who attacked her was dead, and the person who avenged her was in exile, but Tamar's life remained in ruins. Justice that comes through revenge doesn't heal the people it claims to be fighting for.

THE MANIPULATORS

Chapter 14 belongs to the schemers. Joab, David's general, noticed that the king's heart was occupied with thoughts of Absalom. So Joab hired a "wise woman" from a town called Tekoa and coached her to tell David a made-up story. She came to the king claiming to be a widow whose one surviving son had killed his brother. Her family wanted to execute the surviving son for the murder, but that would leave her with no one. Would the king protect him?

David agreed to spare the woman's son. Then she turned the story on him, just as Nathan had done years earlier. If you'll protect my son who killed his brother, she asked, why won't you bring back your own son who did the same thing? Why leave Absalom in exile?

David recognized Joab's fingerprints on the whole scheme. But the argument worked. David told Joab to bring Absalom home.

There was one condition, though: "Let him go to his own house, but he is not to see my face." Absalom could return to Jerusalem, but David wouldn't meet with him. It was a half-measure, neither full justice nor full reconciliation. Absalom was back in the city but banned from the palace. He was close to the king but cut off from him.

BURNING THE FIELDS

For two more years Absalom lived in Jerusalem without seeing his father's face. Eventually he decided to force the issue. He sent messages to Joab, asking for his help again. Joab wouldn't come. So Absalom told his servants to set Joab's barley field on fire.

That got Joab's attention.

Absalom sent Joab to David with a message: "Why did I come back from Geshur? It would be better for me to still be there. Let me see the king's face. And if I'm guilty, let him put me to death."

It was a bold gamble. Absalom was essentially daring David to either fully forgive him or fully punish him. He was betting that David wouldn't execute him, and he was right. David summoned Absalom, and when Absalom bowed before him, the king kissed him.

It looked like reconciliation. But the text gives no indication that any real conversation happened, no confession from Absalom, no discussion of justice, no mention of Tamar. It was a kiss without truth behind it, a gesture without substance. David and Absalom were technically at peace, but nothing had actually been resolved.

And now Absalom was back in Jerusalem, with access to the people, with a reputation for boldness, with smoldering ambition, and with a father who had proven, over and over, that he could be pressured into giving in.

The stage was set for something far worse.

WHAT THIS MEANS FOR US

First, sin's consequences don't stay where you put them. David's sin with Bathsheba didn't just affect David. It echoed into his children's lives. Amnon abused his power the way David had. Absalom plotted murder the way David had. The patterns repeat. The choices we make today can ripple into the lives of the people closest to us in ways we never imagined.

Second, silence in the face of injustice is its own kind of failure. David's refusal to act after Tamar was attacked didn't keep the peace. It guaranteed a worse explosion later. When the people with authority refuse to do what's right, others fill the vacuum, often with methods far more destructive. Sometimes doing nothing is the worst thing you can do.

Third, revenge is not the same as justice. Absalom waited two years and then killed Amnon. It felt like justice, but it wasn't. Justice protects the victim and holds the guilty accountable through proper authority. Revenge satisfies the avenger and usually creates new victims. Amnon's death didn't restore Tamar. It just added another body to the story.

Fourth, being wronged does not give you the right to do wrong. Absalom had legitimate reasons to be furious. What happened to Tamar was horrific, and David's inaction was a disgrace. But Absalom's response, calculated murder followed by years of political scheming, wasn't righteous anger. It was self-serving ambition dressed up as family loyalty. Hurt people can use their pain as an excuse for terrible choices.

Fifth, half-measures don't solve real problems. David's approach to Absalom was a series of incomplete responses: anger without action after Tamar's attack, permission to return without reconciliation, and a kiss without conversation. When we refuse to deal fully with conflict, whether because we're afraid, ashamed, or just tired, we don't prevent disaster. We postpone it.

TALKING POINTS

1. **Tamar begged Amnon to stop, using every argument she could think of.** What does her courage in that moment teach us? And what does Amnon's refusal to listen reveal about the nature of his so-called "love"?

2. **David was furious about what happened to Tamar but did nothing.** Why do you think he was unable to act? Have you ever known the right thing to do but felt unable to do it because of your own past mistakes?

3. **Absalom waited two years before taking revenge.** Why do you think he waited so long? What's the difference between patience and plotting?

4. **Joab used a clever story to convince David to bring Absalom home.** Compare this with how Nathan used a story to confront David about Bathsheba in chapter 12. How were the two stories different in their purpose?

5. **David kissed Absalom, but nothing was truly resolved between them.** What does real reconciliation require that a surface-level gesture doesn't provide? Why is genuine forgiveness so much harder than just moving on?

The fire Nathan had warned about was burning through David's house. A daughter destroyed. A son murdered. Another son in exile for three years, then restored with a kiss that meant nothing. And David, the man after God's own heart, watched it all happen from his throne, paralyzed by his own guilt, unable to be the father or the king his family desperately needed.

But Absalom wasn't finished. The kiss wasn't the end. It was the beginning. He had spent years watching his father's weakness, and now he was going to use it.

Turn the page.

5

THE KING WHO RAN

In Homer's *The Odyssey*, the great king Odysseus is trying to get home. He's been gone from his island kingdom of Ithaca for twenty years, first fighting a war, then lost at sea. While he's away, his palace has been overrun by men who want his throne and his wife. These usurpers eat his food, drink his wine, and act like they own the place. Everyone assumes Odysseus is dead.

But he isn't dead. He's coming home. And the journey back is almost as dangerous as the war itself. Along the way, Odysseus meets people who help him and people who try to destroy him. Some are loyal beyond reason. Others betray him without a second thought. He has to figure out who he can trust, survive impossible odds, and reclaim a kingdom that's been stolen from right under his feet.

When Odysseus finally arrives home, he doesn't walk through the front door in triumph. He comes disguised as a beggar, shuffling through his own halls while strangers mock him. The king of Ithaca, dressed in rags, in his own palace, despised by people who don't know who they're laughing at.

That image, a rightful king driven from his throne and forced to endure humiliation on the road home, is exactly what happens in 2 Samuel 15–19. Except this isn't mythology. It's David. And the person who stole his kingdom wasn't a stranger. It was his own son.

THE THEFT

Absalom spent four years preparing. Every morning he stationed himself at the city gate where people came seeking justice from the king. He would stop them, listen to their complaints, shake his head sympathetically, and say, "Your case is strong, but there's nobody appointed by the king to hear it. If only I were judge, I'd make sure you got justice."

It was brilliant and it was poisonous. Absalom never had to make a single hard decision. He just had to suggest that David wasn't making them either. He played the common man, refusing to let anyone bow to him, pulling people into warm embraces instead. He was charming, handsome, and always available. The text says it plainly: "Absalom stole the hearts of the men of Israel."

When the time was right, Absalom went to Hebron under the pretense of fulfilling a religious vow. From there he sent messengers throughout Israel, and at the sound of a trumpet, his supporters declared him king. The conspiracy was massive. Even Ahithophel, David's most trusted counselor, defected to Absalom's side.

When the news reached David, he didn't stay and fight. He ran.

THE ROAD OUT

David's decision to flee Jerusalem is one of the most surprising moments in the whole story. This was the warrior who killed Goliath, who defeated the Philistines, who conquered Jerusalem in the first place. Why didn't he fight?

The text suggests two reasons. First, David wanted to protect the city. If Absalom attacked Jerusalem, the people would suffer. Second, and more importantly, David seemed to recognize what was happening. Nathan had told him the sword would not depart from his house. Trouble would rise from within his own family. This was it. David didn't fight because, at some level, he accepted that this disaster was the consequence of his own sin.

But acceptance didn't mean despair. As David left Jerusalem, the road became a test of faith, and David met it with a trust in God that might be the most impressive thing he ever did.

The first person he encountered was Ittai, a foreign soldier from Gath who had only recently joined David's service. David told him to go back. Why share the exile of a king who might never return? Ittai's answer was stunning: "As the Lord lives, and as my lord the king lives, wherever my lord the king shall be, whether for death or for life, there also will your servant be." David had lost his throne, but he hadn't lost everyone.

Next came the priests, Zadok and Abiathar, carrying the ark of the covenant. They were ready to bring God's presence into exile with David. But David sent the ark back. His words reveal a faith that had been tested to its core and come out clean: "If I find favor in the eyes of the Lord, he will bring me back and let me see both it and his dwelling place. But if he says, 'I have no pleasure in you,' here I am, let him do to me what seems good to him."

No manipulation. No trying to use God as a bargaining chip. David put himself entirely in God's hands. If God wanted to restore him, he would. If not, David would accept that too. It was the purest expression of faith David ever uttered.

Then David sent his friend Hushai back into the city as a spy, to counter the advice of Ahithophel from the inside. Even in his deepest submission to God, David used his head. Trusting God and taking practical action weren't contradictions. They were partners.

CURSES AND KINDNESS

The road down from Jerusalem brought more encounters. Ziba, the servant of Mephibosheth, showed up with donkeys loaded with food and wine, claiming that Mephibosheth had stayed behind hoping the rebellion would restore Saul's dynasty. David, in the chaos of the moment, gave Ziba everything that belonged to Mephibosheth. It was a hasty decision he would later regret.

Then came Shimei, a relative of Saul's family. As David's group passed along the road, Shimei followed on the ridge above, throwing rocks and dirt and screaming curses. "Get out! Get out, you man of blood! The Lord has paid you back for all the blood of the house of Saul!" David's men wanted to kill him. Abishai offered to cut off his head on the spot.

David said no. "If he is cursing because the Lord has said to him, 'Curse David,' who then shall say, 'Why have you done so?'" And then David said something remarkable: "It may be that the Lord will look on my affliction, and the Lord will repay me with good for his cursing today."

Even under a shower of rocks and insults, David held on to the possibility that God's grace was bigger than his punishment. He didn't know for certain. He said "it may be." But the fact that he could even imagine such a God, a God who might look at guilt and return blessing, tells you everything about what David believed about the Lord's character.

THE BATTLE OF THE COUNSELORS

Back in Jerusalem, a battle was being fought with words instead of swords. Ahithophel, the defector, gave Absalom advice that was militarily perfect: pursue David immediately with a small, fast force, catch him while he's exhausted, kill him alone, and the war is over.

The plan would have worked. David would have been dead.

But Absalom made a fateful decision. He asked Hushai for a second opinion. Hushai, David's spy, knew exactly what he needed to do. He didn't just disagree with Ahithophel's plan. He appealed to Absalom's vanity. "Don't send someone else to do this," Hushai argued. "Gather all of Israel and lead them yourself. Personally." He painted a picture of Absalom riding at the head of a massive army, crushing David with overwhelming force. It was terrible military advice, but it was irresistible to a man who loved being at the center of everything.

Absalom chose Hushai's plan. And the narrator tells us why in the most important sentence of the entire rebellion: "For the Lord had ordained to defeat the good counsel of Ahithophel, so that the Lord might bring harm upon Absalom."

Behind the scheming and the speeches, behind the politics and the power plays, God was at work. Absalom thought he was making a free decision. Hushai thought he was being clever. But God was the one steering the outcome. The kingdom that belonged to David would not be taken from him. Not by his son. Not by the smartest counselor in Israel. Not by anyone.

When Ahithophel saw that his advice had been rejected, he knew what it meant. The rebellion would fail. He went home, put his affairs in order, and hanged himself. He was the Judas of the Old Testament, a trusted insider who betrayed the Lord's anointed and came to a terrible end.

THE FOREST AND THE TREE

David's forces met Absalom's army in the forest of Ephraim, east of the Jordan. Before the battle, David gave his commanders one instruction that reveals the war raging inside his own heart: "Deal gently for my sake with the young man Absalom."

The father in David wanted his son spared. But the God who had ordained Absalom's defeat had other plans.

The battle was a rout. Absalom's army was shattered. Twenty thousand men fell that day, and the dense forest claimed more lives than the sword. In the chaos, Absalom himself was riding his mule through the trees when his head caught in the thick branches of a great oak. The mule kept going. Absalom was left hanging, alive but helpless, suspended between heaven and earth.

Joab was told about it. Despite David's explicit order, Joab took three javelins and plunged them into Absalom's chest while he hung in the tree. His armor-bearers finished the job.

They threw Absalom's body into a pit in the forest and piled stones over it.

The rebellion was over. The kingdom was saved. And David's son was dead.

MY SON, MY SON

David was waiting at the gate of Mahanaim when the runners arrived. The first brought news of victory but dodged the question David cared about most. Then a second messenger arrived and told the whole truth.

David's response is one of the most heartbreaking moments in all of Scripture: "O my son Absalom, my son, my son Absalom! Would I had died instead of you, O Absalom, my son, my son!"

The man who had sung a lament for Saul and Jonathan, who had wept for Abner, who had grieved over his infant son, now collapsed under a grief heavier than all the others combined. This wasn't just a father losing a child. This was a father who knew, deep in his bones, that his own sin had set the chain of events in motion. Nathan had said the sword would not leave his house. Amnon was dead. Now Absalom. David knew he deserved the punishment. But knowing that didn't make the grief any lighter.

David's mourning was so intense that it turned the army's victory into a funeral. Soldiers who had risked their lives to save the kingdom slunk back into camp like men who had done something shameful. Joab confronted David bluntly: "You love those who hate you and hate those who love you. If Absalom were alive and all of us were dead, you'd be pleased."

It was harsh. It was partially unfair. But it was also the jolt David needed. He pulled himself together and went out to acknowledge his troops.

THE LONG WALK HOME

David's return to Jerusalem mirrored his departure. The same cast of characters reappeared, and David had to decide what to do with each of them.

Shimei, the man who had cursed and thrown rocks, arrived first, falling on his face, begging for mercy. David spared him, though his men wanted blood.

Mephibosheth came next, unwashed, unkempt, looking like a man who had been grieving since the day David left. He explained that Ziba had lied about him, had taken advantage of his disability to steal his inheritance and slander him to the king. David, perhaps too weary or politically cautious to investigate, split the estate between them. It was expedient but not just.

Barzillai, an elderly, wealthy farmer who had provided for David's entire camp during the exile, came to say goodbye. David offered him a place at court. The old man politely declined. He was eighty years old, he said. He could barely taste his food. What good would palace life do him now? He asked only to go home and die near the graves of his parents. His contentment was as striking as Absalom's ambition had been hollow.

The return was not triumphant. There was bickering between the northern and southern tribes over who got to escort the king home. The seeds of future division were already sprouting. David had his kingdom back, but it was bruised, fractured, and soaked in the blood of his own family.

WHAT THIS MEANS FOR US

First, trusting God doesn't mean doing nothing. David submitted completely to God's will but still sent Hushai as a spy and organized his forces for battle. Faith and action work together. Trusting that God is in control frees you to use your mind and take wise steps without the panicked belief that everything depends on you.

Second, God works behind the scenes even when you can't see him. The defeat of Ahithophel's counsel looked like a lucky break. It was actually God steering the outcome. In the middle of your worst season, God may be working in ways you won't recognize until much later.

Third, consequences are real, even for the forgiven. David was forgiven for his sin with Bathsheba. But the consequences played out in his family for the rest of his life. Grace doesn't always remove the wreckage. Sometimes it carries you through it.

Fourth, grief and gratitude can exist at the same time. David's kingdom was saved and his son was dead. Those two realities sat side by side, and neither erased the other. Life is sometimes like that. You can thank God for what he's done and still weep over what it cost.

Fifth, the real enemy of God's kingdom will never win. Absalom had the army, the counselor, and the popularity. God had a spy, a forest, and a plan. The kingdom that God establishes cannot be overthrown, no matter how impressive the opposition looks.

TALKING POINTS

1. **David sent the ark back to Jerusalem and said, "If I find favor in the eyes of the Lord, he will bring me back."** What does this teach us about the difference between trusting God and trying to control God?

2. **Ittai the foreigner refused to leave David's side, even though he had no obligation to stay.** What does his loyalty teach us about commitment to people and causes that matter, even when the outcome is uncertain?

3. **Absalom's rebellion succeeded because he told people what they wanted to hear.** How can we learn to recognize the difference between leaders who truly care and leaders who are just working the crowd?

4. **David told his commanders to "deal gently" with Absalom, but Joab killed him anyway.** Was Joab right or wrong? How do you weigh a father's love against the demands of justice and the safety of a nation?

5. **David cried, "Would I had died instead of you, O Absalom, my son!"** What fueled the depth of David's grief? How does guilt complicate sorrow? And is there anyone who actually did die in our place?

The kingdom was saved. The rebellion was crushed. The rightful king was back on his throne. But David walked through the gates of Jerusalem a different man than the one who had fled through them. He had trusted God in the wilderness and found God faithful. He had also buried another son and learned again that grace does not always mean the absence of pain.

The story of David's reign was drawing to a close. But the promise God made to him, the promise of a throne that would last forever, was just getting started.

Turn the page.

6

STILL STANDING

In Disney's *The Jungle Book*, a young boy named Mowgli is trying to survive in a world that seems designed to destroy him. He doesn't belong in the jungle, and the jungle knows it. The tiger Shere Khan wants him dead. The snake Kaa tries to hypnotize and devour him. The monkeys kidnap him. Even the journey to the man-village, where Mowgli might finally be safe, is one long obstacle course of dangers he barely escapes.

But here's the thing: Mowgli keeps surviving. Not because he's the strongest or the smartest creature in the jungle. He survives because allies keep showing up at the right moment. Baloo fights off the monkeys. Bagheera watches over him through the night. The vultures rally when Shere Khan finally attacks. Mowgli is small and vulnerable, but something keeps him alive through every threat.

That's a picture of David's kingdom in 2 Samuel 20–21. By this point in the story, the kingdom has been through more than anyone could have predicted. Absalom's rebellion nearly destroyed it. David's own sin scarred it. The nation is bruised, fractured, and exhausted. And yet more threats keep coming.

Another rebellion. An ancient wrong that brings a devastating famine. Giant warriors from the old Philistine enemy. It's one crisis after another, like a boxer who keeps getting hit but won't go down.

The kingdom of David is still standing. Not because David is invincible, but because the God who established that kingdom refuses to let it fall.

ANOTHER REBELLION

David had barely crossed back into Jerusalem after Absalom's revolt when the next crisis erupted. During the journey home, the northern tribes and the tribe of Judah had been bickering over who had the right to escort the king. It was petty and political, but it was dangerous, because it exposed a fault line that ran through the heart of the nation.

A man named Sheba saw his chance. Sheba was from the tribe of Benjamin, Saul's old tribe, and the text calls him a "worthless man." He blew a trumpet and shouted a rallying cry that would echo for centuries in Israel's history: "We have no portion in David! Every man to his tents, O Israel!"

Just like that, the northern tribes peeled away and followed Sheba. The nation that had just reunited after Absalom's rebellion was splitting apart again. David was left with Judah.

David acted quickly. He ordered Amasa, his new military commander, to mobilize the troops within three days. Amasa was too slow. So David sent Abishai with the standing army to chase Sheba before the revolt could gain momentum.

But Joab had his own plans. When the army caught up with Amasa at Gibeon, Joab greeted him like a friend, reached for his beard as if to kiss him, and stabbed him in the stomach with a concealed sword. Amasa died in the road. Joab stepped over the body and took command of the army as if nothing had happened.

It was the third time Joab had murdered someone in cold blood: first Abner, then Absalom, now Amasa. Each time, Joab did it to protect his own position. Each time, David was unable or unwilling to stop him. Joab was fiercely loyal to David's throne but completely unsubmissive to David's authority. He served the king while acting as his own king.

Sheba, meanwhile, had fled to the far north of Israel, to a city called Abel Beth-maacah, where he holed up behind the walls. Joab arrived and began battering the city to rubble.

Then a voice rose above the noise of the siege.

THE WOMAN WHO SAVED A CITY

A woman inside the city called out to Joab from the wall. She identified herself and her town's reputation: Abel was known as a place of wisdom, a city where people came to settle disputes peacefully. "I am one of those who are peaceable and faithful in Israel," she told Joab. "Why will you swallow up the heritage of the Lord?"

Joab explained: he didn't want to destroy the city. He wanted one man, Sheba, who had rebelled against King David. "Hand him over, and I'll leave."

The woman made a promise: "His head will be thrown to you over the wall."

She went back to her people and persuaded them. Sheba was killed. His head came over the wall. Joab blew the trumpet, the army dispersed, and the city was saved. One unnamed woman, armed with nothing but courage and good sense, accomplished what an army couldn't. She saved an entire city from destruction by cutting the problem down to its actual size: this wasn't about wiping out a town, it was about one rebellious man.

The chapter closes with a list of David's officials, quietly confirming that, despite everything, the government was still functioning. Joab, predictably, was back in command of the army. The kingdom was intact. Battered, but intact.

THE SADNESS THAT LINGERED

Before the pursuit of Sheba, the narrator pauses on a detail that's easy to overlook but impossible to forget once you see it. When David returned to Jerusalem, one of the first things he did was deal with the ten concubines he had left behind to care for the palace, the same women Absalom had publicly violated during his rebellion.

David put them in a guarded house. He provided for them. But he never went to see them again. They lived the rest of their lives in confinement, "as if in widowhood." They had done nothing wrong. They were victims of Absalom's cruelty and, before that, of David's sin, since Nathan had prophesied that exactly this would happen. Their lives had been turned to gray because of the choices of powerful men around them.

The writer doesn't editorialize. He doesn't tell you how to feel. He just shows you these women locked away and lets the sadness sink in. Sometimes the consequences of sin land on people who never made the choice. And sometimes there's no way to undo it.

A FAMINE AND A BROKEN OATH

Chapter 21 takes us to a different crisis entirely. A famine struck Israel and lasted three years. This wasn't a random drought. When David sought God's face, the answer came: "There is bloodguilt on Saul and on his house, because he put the Gibeonites to death."

To understand this, you have to go back to the book of Joshua. When the Israelites first entered the Promised Land, the Gibeonites tricked Israel's leaders into making a peace treaty with them. It was sworn in God's name, which made it permanently binding. Even though the Gibeonites had lied to get the treaty, the oath was real. God's name had been invoked, and that meant the agreement could not be broken.

But Saul, in a burst of misguided national pride, had tried to wipe out the Gibeonites. He violated the ancient oath. He broke a promise sworn in God's name. And even though Saul was now dead, the guilt remained. The land was suffering because a covenant had been shattered.

This is one of the hardest passages in 2 Samuel. David asked the Gibeonites what would satisfy them. They didn't want money. They asked for seven of Saul's descendants to be handed over and executed. David agreed. He selected seven men from Saul's family and gave them to the Gibeonites, who put them to death.

But David spared Mephibosheth, Jonathan's son, because of the covenant he had made with Jonathan. Even in the middle of this grim crisis, David kept his promise. Saul had been a covenant-breaker. David would be a covenant-keeper.

THE MOTHER WHO WOULDN'T LEAVE

What comes next is one of the most haunting scenes in the Bible. A woman named Rizpah, the mother of two of the men who were executed, took a piece of rough sackcloth and spread it on a rock near where the bodies had been left exposed. Then she sat down. And she stayed.

Day after day. Week after week. She guarded the bodies of her sons from the birds that circled by day and the animals that prowled by night. She couldn't bring them back. She couldn't undo what had happened. But she could do this one thing: she could protect what was left of them from being torn apart.

The text doesn't tell us how long she kept her vigil. It only says she stayed "from the beginning of harvest until rain fell upon them from the heavens," when the famine finally broke and God's anger was turned away.

When David heard what Rizpah had done, he was moved to action. He gathered the bones of Saul and Jonathan from Jabesh-gilead, where they had been buried after the battle of Gilboa, and he collected the remains of the seven who had been executed. He buried them all together in the family tomb of Saul's father, Kish, in the land of Benjamin.

Then the narrator gives us the bottom line: "After that, God responded to the plea for the land." The famine ended. The crisis passed. But the image of Rizpah sitting on that rock, keeping her terrible watch, stays with you long after you turn the page.

The writer doesn't rush past this. He wants you to feel it. He wants you to understand that broken covenants produce real suffering, that the wages of sin are paid in real lives, and that sometimes the only faithful response to something you cannot fix is simply to stay and bear witness to the cost.

THE LAMP OF ISRAEL

The chapter ends with four short battle reports from David's wars against the Philistines. These snippets come from various points in David's reign, grouped here not by chronology but by theme: each one involves a descendant of an ancient race of giants, the Rephaim, fighting for the Philistines.

In the first, David himself was in the thick of the fighting when he grew exhausted. A giant named Ishbi-benob, armed with a massive bronze spear, moved in for the kill. David would have died if Abishai hadn't stepped in and cut the giant down.

After that close call, David's men made him swear an oath: "You shall no longer go out with us to battle, lest you quench the lamp of Israel." They called David the lamp of Israel because without him the nation would be plunged into darkness. Protecting the king wasn't just about one man's life. It was about the survival of everything God had built through him.

Three more giant-killers follow in quick succession. Sibbecai killed a giant named Saph. Elhanan killed another Philistine champion. And Jonathan, David's nephew, killed a towering warrior with six fingers on each hand and six toes on each foot, a man who made the mistake of mocking Israel just as Goliath had done years earlier. He met the same end.

The summary verse ties it all together: "These four were descended from the giants in Gath, and they fell by the hand of David and by the hand of his servants."

The Philistines had been Israel's most dangerous enemy

for generations. God had promised that David would deliver Israel from them. And here, in these brief battle reports, that promise is confirmed. Every giant fell. Every threat was answered. What began in the Valley of Elah with a shepherd boy and a sling was completed by David's warriors in these scattered skirmishes. God finishes what he starts.

WHAT THIS MEANS FOR US

First, God's kingdom survives what should destroy it. Sheba's revolt, Joab's treachery, a three-year famine, Philistine giants, one crisis after another crashed against David's kingdom. None of them toppled it. The kingdom that God establishes may look fragile. It isn't. It survives because God sustains it, not because its human leaders are flawless.

Second, broken promises have real and lasting consequences. Saul violated an oath sworn in God's name, and the consequences outlasted his life by decades. God takes promises seriously, especially promises made in his name. The famine didn't arrive because God was petty. It arrived because his name had been dishonored, and that dishonor had to be addressed.

Third, faithfulness in small things matters enormously. Rizpah couldn't undo what had been done to her sons. But she could sit on that rock and guard their remains. Her small, stubborn act of love moved a king to action. You may not be able to fix the big things. But the faithful thing you can do, however small, may matter more than you know.

Fourth, God protects the people who carry his promise. David was the lamp of Israel, the king through whom God's promise would continue. When Ishbi-benob nearly killed him, Abishai was there. God doesn't let the bearers of his promise be snuffed out before his purposes are complete. That's true for David, and it's true for everyone who belongs to God.

Fifth, every enemy of God's people will eventually be silenced. The giants who mocked Israel met the same fate as Goliath. The rebellions that threatened the kingdom were crushed. The pattern is consistent throughout Scripture: those who oppose God's purposes don't get the last word. Ever.

TALKING POINTS

1. **Sheba's revolt happened because of tribal bickering that spiraled out of control.** How can small disagreements between people who should be united lead to serious divisions? What can be done to prevent that?
2. **The concubines in 20:3 suffered lifelong consequences for something that wasn't their fault.** How should we respond when we see innocent people paying the price for someone else's choices?
3. **The wise woman of Abel saved her city with words, not weapons.** What does her example teach us about the power of clear thinking and courageous speech in a crisis?
4. **Rizpah's vigil over her sons' remains is one of the most heartbreaking scenes in the Bible.** What do you think the writer wants us to feel when we read it? Why does he linger on this scene instead of rushing past it?
5. **David's men called him "the lamp of Israel."** What does that metaphor mean? And who is the ultimate "lamp" that can never be quenched?

The kingdom had survived another round of threats. Rebellions crushed. Giants killed. A famine ended. A broken covenant addressed. The list of David's officials stood as quiet proof that the government was still functioning, still serving, still in place.

But David was getting old. His strength was fading. The man who once killed a lion with his bare hands now needed his soldiers to fight his battles for him. The lamp of Israel was flickering.

What David needed to do, before that lamp went out, was look back at everything God had done and look forward to everything God had promised. And that is exactly what he did.

Turn the page.

7

THE LAST WORD

In Ernest Hemingway's *The Old Man and the Sea*, an aging fisherman named Santiago hasn't caught a fish in eighty-four days. The other fishermen feel sorry for him. The boy who used to help him has been pulled away by his parents. Santiago rows out alone into the Gulf Stream, hooks the largest marlin anyone has ever seen, and fights it for three days and three nights. His hands cramp. The line cuts into his skin. The sun blisters his back. He talks to the fish. He talks to himself. He talks to God.

When he finally kills the marlin and lashes it to his boat, the sharks come. One by one they tear at his prize, and Santiago fights them off with everything he has, a harpoon, a knife, a club, the broken tiller. By the time he reaches the harbor, the marlin is nothing but a skeleton. The other fishermen stare. Santiago drags himself home and falls asleep.

But here's what matters: Santiago is not defeated. He lost the fish, but he proved something about who he is and whose he is. He endured. And when the boy sees him the next morning, bandaged and broken and sleeping, the boy weeps, because he knows what the old man went through and he knows the old man never quit.

The final chapters of 2 Samuel are David's version of that story. An aging king, battered by decades of battles, betrayals, and consequences, looks back over everything he's been through and opens his mouth. Not to complain. Not to make excuses. Not to rewrite history. To sing. To worship the God who carried him through every danger, every failure, and every enemy. And then to point forward, past his own flawed reign, to a coming King who will get it right.

These are David's last words. And they are not about David. They are about God.

THE SONG

Second Samuel 22 is a psalm, nearly identical to Psalm 18. It's David's longest prayer in the Bible, fifty-one verses of worship pouring out of a man who has survived what should have killed him a hundred times over.

The heading tells us when David composed it: after God had delivered him from all his enemies and from Saul. This isn't a song written in the middle of the fight. It's a song written by a man sitting safely at the end of a long, brutal journey, looking back over all of it, and realizing that the only explanation for his survival is God.

David doesn't start slowly. He erupts. "The Lord is my rock and my fortress and my deliverer, my God, my rock, in whom I take refuge, my shield, the horn of my salvation, my stronghold and my refuge, my savior." He piles up words because no single word is big enough. He's trying to say something his language can't contain: God is everything to me, and I can't say it loud enough.

Then David explains why his praise is so intense. He describes the danger he lived through, using the language of drowning: waves of death surrounded him, torrents of destruction overwhelmed him, the cords of the grave coiled around him. This wasn't a figure of speech. David spent years running from a king who wanted him dead. He hid in caves, fled to enemy territory, watched friends die, nearly lost his mind. Death dogged him daily. And every single time, he cried out to God, and God answered.

But David doesn't just say God answered. He describes what God's rescue looked like from the inside, and the picture is staggering. The earth trembled. The foundations of the heavens shook. Smoke rose from God's nostrils. He parted the heavens and came down. He rode on the wings of the wind. He shot arrows of lightning and scattered David's enemies. He reached down from on high and drew David out of deep waters.

Did earthquakes literally happen every time David escaped Saul? No. But David isn't writing a news report. He's writing poetry, and the poetry tells a deeper truth than any report could: the God who rescued David was the same God who shook Mount Sinai, the same God who split the Red Sea, the same God who made the heavens. Every small deliverance in David's life was backed by the full, terrifying, world-shaking power of the Creator.

That is why David's praise is so intense. He isn't just grateful for a lucky break. He's overwhelmed by the God behind every break.

The second half of the song shifts from deliverance to dominion. David praises God for making him king, for giving him victory over nations, for establishing a kingdom that stretches far beyond Israel's borders. But the credit never lands on David. "You armed me with strength for battle." "You gave me the shield of your salvation." "You made my enemies turn their backs." Every victory belongs to God.

David closes the song with a word that points far beyond his own reign: "He shows steadfast love to his anointed, to David and his offspring forever." That word "forever" reaches past David's lifetime, past Solomon, past the exile, all the way to a stable in Bethlehem. The song ends where the promise always ends: with a kingdom that will never fall.

THE PROPHECY

Chapter 23 opens with what the Bible calls "the last words of David." Not the last words he ever spoke, but his last recorded oracle, his final message as the anointed king and prophet of Israel.

David introduces himself carefully. He's "the man who was raised up high, the anointed of the God of Jacob, the sweet singer of Israel." He wants you to know that what he's about to say isn't opinion. It's revelation. "The Spirit of the Lord speaks through me; his word is on my tongue. The God of Israel has spoken; the Rock of Israel has said to me…"

And then comes the prophecy: a ruler is coming. A ruler over all people, not just Israel. A ruler who is righteous. A ruler who governs in the fear of God. And his reign will be like the morning sun rising on a cloudless day, like the brightness after rain that makes the grass spring up from the earth.

That image is everything. After all the darkness of 2 Samuel, the rebellions, the murders, the broken families, the consequences that never stopped coming, David's final vision is of light. Morning. Sunshine after rain. New growth. The promise isn't that David's dynasty will simply continue. The promise is that a King is coming whose reign will actually heal the world.

David knew he wasn't that king. He'd failed too often and too badly. But he also knew that the covenant God had made with him was real, "an everlasting covenant, ordered in all things and secure." He was confident that what God had promised, God would do.

The prophecy ends with a warning: those who refuse this coming King, the "godless" who want no part of a righteous ruler's reign, will be like thorns tossed away and burned. David's last prophetic word includes both an invitation and a boundary. The kingdom is coming. It will be glorious. But it will not include those who reject it.

THE WARRIORS

Sandwiched between David's song and his final failure is a section that might seem like an interruption: the list of David's mighty men. Thirty-seven warriors, named one by one, with brief accounts of their extraordinary deeds.

Josheb-basshebeth killed eight hundred men in a single battle. Eleazar fought the Philistines until his hand froze to his sword. Shammah stood alone in a field of lentils when everyone else ran and defended it single-handedly. Three unnamed warriors broke through a Philistine garrison just to bring David a drink of water from the well at Bethlehem, a drink David refused to swallow because he said it was too costly, pouring it out before the Lord instead.

These weren't sidekicks. They were the men who bled with David through every season of his reign. They fought Philistines, survived Absalom's rebellion, and stood by the king when others betrayed him. The list is the Bible's way of saying that David didn't do any of this alone. God works through communities of faithful people, not just solitary heroes.

And buried in the list, almost as a footnote, is a name that cuts like a knife: "Uriah the Hittite." The man David murdered. Still listed among the mighty men. Still honored. The Bible doesn't erase what David did to him, even in a passage celebrating David's warriors.

THE LAST FAILURE

If 2 Samuel ended with the song and the prophecy, it would feel like a triumph. But the book has one more chapter, and it's not triumphant at all.

David ordered a census of Israel. On the surface, this might not seem like a big deal, just a king counting his people. But something about it was deeply wrong. Even Joab, not exactly a man of spiritual sensitivity, tried to talk David out of it. "May the Lord your God multiply the people a hundred times over," Joab said, "but why does my lord the king delight in this thing?"

The text doesn't spell out exactly what made the census sinful. But the most likely explanation is that David was counting his military strength, measuring his kingdom by its numbers rather than trusting the God who had built it. After a lifetime of depending on God, David slipped into depending on what he could see and count. It was a quiet, subtle form of pride, the kind that replaces trust in God with trust in resources.

After the census was completed, David's conscience hit him like a hammer. "I have sinned greatly in what I have done. But now, O Lord, please take away the guilt of your servant, for I have done very foolishly."

God sent the prophet Gad with three options for discipline: three years of famine, three months fleeing from enemies, or three days of plague. David's answer reveals a man who, even in his worst moments, still understood God better than most people ever will: "Let us fall into the hand of the Lord, for his mercy is great; but let me not fall into the hand of man."

David chose to fall into God's hands. Even God's discipline, David believed, would be wrapped in mercy. And he was right.

The plague struck Israel. Seventy thousand people died. But when the destroying angel reached Jerusalem, God stopped him. "Enough! Withdraw your hand." The angel was standing at the threshing floor of a man named Araunah.

Gad told David to build an altar there. David went to Araunah and offered to buy the threshing floor. Araunah offered to give it to him for free, along with oxen for the sacrifice. But David refused: "I will not offer burnt offerings to the Lord my God that cost me nothing."

David paid full price. He built the altar. He offered sacrifices. And the plague stopped. The wrath of God was turned away through an offering made at a specific place, purchased at a real cost, by a king who knew he deserved judgment but trusted in a God whose mercy is greater than his anger.

Here's what makes this ending extraordinary: that threshing floor, the exact spot where the angel stopped and the altar was built, became the location where Solomon would later build the temple. The place of David's last failure became the place of Israel's greatest worship. The spot where judgment halted became the spot where God's presence would dwell among his people for generations.

WHAT THIS MEANS FOR US

First, the right response to a lifetime of God's faithfulness is worship. David looked back on decades of danger, failure, and rescue and his instinct was to sing. Not to brag about what he'd accomplished, but to pile up every word he could find for the God who had carried him. If you can look back on your life and see even one moment where God came through, you have reason to worship.

Second, God's coming kingdom will heal what this world has broken. David's prophecy of a righteous ruler whose reign is like sunshine after rain is the Bible's promise that things will not always be the way they are now. Injustice will end. Brokenness will be mended. The King who is coming will not fail the way every human leader has. That hope is meant to sustain you through every dark chapter of your own story.

Third, even the best people need grace until their very last day. David sinned with the census at the end of his life, proving that spiritual maturity doesn't make you immune to foolishness. You will need God's mercy tomorrow as much as you needed it yesterday. Never stop asking for it.

Fourth, falling into God's hands is always the safest place to be. David chose God's discipline over human opposition because he knew God's character. Even when God is angry, his mercy is great. Even when he disciplines, he does it as a father who loves his children. If you must fall, fall toward God.

Fifth, God turns places of failure into places of worship. The threshing floor where judgment stopped became the site of the temple. The cross where Jesus died became the source of the world's salvation. God has an extraordinary habit of taking the worst thing that ever happened and making it the foundation for the best thing that ever will.

TALKING POINTS

1. **David's song in chapter 22 uses dramatic poetry to describe God's rescue.** Why do you think David chose poetry instead of just listing the facts? What does this teach us about how to worship?

2. **David's "last words" describe a coming King whose reign is like sunshine after rain.** What would a world look like under a perfectly righteous ruler? What are you most looking forward to about that future?

3. **The list of David's mighty men includes Uriah the Hittite.** Why do you think the Bible includes his name here, even after what David did to him? What does that tell us about God's view of Uriah?

4. **David said, "I will not offer burnt offerings to the Lord my God that cost me nothing."** What does it mean to give God something that actually costs you? What might that look like in your own life?

5. **The threshing floor where God's judgment stopped became the site of the temple.** Can you think of other places in the Bible, or in your own experience, where God turned a place of pain into something beautiful?

The book of 2 Samuel ends with an altar, a sacrifice, and the wrath of God turned away. It ends with David on his knees, spending his own money, offering worship that costs him something, at the exact spot where his greatest descendant's temple will one day stand.

It's a fitting ending for a book that has been, from first page to last, about the relentless faithfulness of God to a deeply flawed king. David danced and David fell. He sang psalms and he schemed murders. He showed breathtaking faith and staggering foolishness, sometimes in the same chapter. He was the man after God's own heart, not because he was perfect but because every time he was broken, he turned back to God. Every single time.

And through it all, the promise held. The covenant God made with David in chapter 7, the promise of a throne that would last forever, survived David's adultery, Absalom's rebellion, three-year famines, and plagues that killed thousands. Nothing could kill that promise, because it didn't depend on David. It depended on God.

A thousand years later, in the same city where David built his altar, another Son of David would hang on a cross. The wrath of God would fall again, not on seventy thousand, but on one. And when it was finished, when the sacrifice had been made and the price had been paid, the mercy David sang about would flood the entire world.

David's story is over. But the promise he carried is alive. It's alive in every church that gathers to worship. It's alive in every person who has fallen into the hands of the Lord and discovered that his mercies are many. It's alive in the King who came, who died, who rose, and who is coming back to reign in righteousness, like the light of morning when the sun rises, a morning without clouds.

The shepherd boy became a king. The king became a sinner. The sinner became a worshiper. And the God who chose him never let him go.

That's the story of 2 Samuel. And if you belong to David's God, it's your story too.

www.ingramcontent.com/pod-product-compliance
Ingram Content Group UK Ltd.
Pitfield, Milton Keynes, MK11 3LW, UK
UKHW020420250726
13967UKWH00007B/2745